THE
CELLULITE
PROPHECY

Printed in the United States of America
First Printing: January 1995
Second Printing: March 1995

light-hearted books is a registered trademark of Lumina.
For information, contact
Lumina Publishing
501 Wisteria Road
Daytona Beach, FL 32118
(904) 258-5300

ISBN 0-9645015-0-3

THE CELLULITE PROPHECY

An Adventure

'AUTHOR UNKNOWN'

light-hearted books
a division of **Lumina**

Dedicated

to
Edith and Murray Rubin,
embodiments of love, light and beauty

Acknowledgment

With gratitude and thanks to James Redfield
for his loving
contribution to global consciousness

CONTENTS

UNKNOWN AUTHOR'S NOTE

For half a century now, a new question has been entering the human consciousness: just what *is* reality? When I was very little, Jane Fonda seemed big, up on the silver screen. But today, *she's* small and *I'm* the big one: my girth has expanded along with my consciousness, perhaps at even a greater rate. Reality keeps shifting. If you find yourself reading this book, then perhaps you sense some coincidence which has meaning to someone.

It begins with a heightened perception that breathing has become difficult when your shirt is fully buttoned. We seek higher meaning in this but probably can't find it.

We know that life is a great unfolding process. But we know something else as well: our waistlines seem to be a part of this process. Why do so many of us who are raising our consciousness— men *and* women alike— have bodies that are some amount bigger than we'd like them to be?

The following story is offered toward a new understanding. If it inspires you, if something within you says "there *is* hope!," then pass on your enthusiasm to another, and another, and allow the psychological contagion to happen— but also suggest to them that it's better to get their own copy than to try to receive it verbally from you.

All that any of us have to do is suspend some of our over-eating and under-exercising just long enough....

A
MORE CRITICAL
MASS

I drove up to the restaurant and loosened my belt, awaiting Charlene's arrival. Why had she chosen this restaurant after we hadn't eaten together for 6 years?

I was anticipating seeing what kind of shape Charlene was in— and what about that manuscript she had mentioned over the phone? God.... she indicated that a mysterious document exists somewhere that could help me resolve the reality that my physical self had expanded much more than my spiritual self for most of my life, and I had become a big person. I just hadn't been able to find peace— feeling unable to correlate my overweight-ness with my spiritual quest. For years, I'd been seeking the higher wisdom on this to help set my soul free.

When we finally met, it was great. She had the same chubby appearance, but her eyes were filled with light.

"Charlene, can we talk about this manuscript first?" I blurted out, suddenly aware of how eager I must have sounded.

"Well... sure.... Can I at least ask how you are?"

1

I looked at her, now feeling ridiculous.

"Oh, I'm sorry for being rude. I'm fine. It's just that you piqued my interest in this new find...."

She smiled and reached down for an envelope.

"For years I'd heard rumors of an ancient manuscript that had been found in Peru, but couldn't find anyone who would admit to knowing anything about it."

She paused.

"Then, by great coincidence, or so it seemed, I met a priest in my Weight Consciousness group who had been in Peru and had actually seen it. I was overjoyed! He told me that the Manuscript has eight segments— or Insights— which have been found so far, and that they offered a higher truth for us weight-challenged-and-on-the-spiritual-path. A ninth Insight is rumored to exist."

Just then, a few tables away, a woman must have lost her mind, because she suddenly shouted at her companion:

"You chose this lousy place! The food stinks, just like our relationship! Absolutely nothing is going right in my life! Father in heaven, step forth and guide me!"

With that the heavy-set woman ran from the room in tears.

Charlene's eyes opened wide.

"Did you see that? The First Insight spoke of a distended feeling that many people on the earth plane would begin to experience as we head toward the year 2000. I had noticed that woman go to the salad bar and fill up a large plate at least twice, and that, of course, all before the entree came. I think that she was experiencing the uneasiness mentioned in the Manuscript and she took it out on her partner."

"What exactly does the Manuscript say?" I asked.

"He told me the Manuscript says the number of people who are conscious of their waistlines reaching critical mass will *itself* reach a critical mass— more and more people becoming larger and larger until, at the end of the twentieth century, we will fill up the earth. He said this was not an overpopulation problem. The problem will be that most of the existing population will be busting out of their pants... but that this situation is actually a great opportunity for those people to— in some way— transform the planet.

"The priest went on to say that every coincidence was important, and that most things were coincidences. He then said that it's our *awareness* of coincidences that's the most important thing of all, and that everything's going to be all right everywhere eventually."

I sat quietly for several moments before speaking. "I may be missing the whole point you're making, but this very meeting with you is coincidental in a way. We ordered peach melba for dessert the *last* time we were here, too."

That evening I contemplated my interesting day, but I was skeptical. I had been caught up in the social idealism of the Sixties and Seventies, and even in the spiritual interests of the Eighties. And now I listened to a station that played music of the Forties, Fifties, Sixties, Seventies, Eighties and Nineties. But I was still fat, so what did it all really mean?

I awoke the next morning with almost total recall of a dream—and a big desire to make some pancakes and blueberries. I was relieved that I was able to prepare breakfast and process the dream at the same time. In the dream, I was at the largest salad bar you could ever imagine—it was extremely surreal. I felt completely lost as it was immense, and I needed guidance. By coincidence, if that's what it was, I was guided to where everything was, including items I had never tasted before. I couldn't tell where I was or what anything meant. But I did feel wonderful after waking up from that dream.

The weather outside was beautiful. I decided to go for a swim in the lake, but felt fatigued after just a few strokes—I was hauling a lot more weight now than I used to when I'd visit my grandfather as a younger person.

I wondered if I was receiving inner guidance to go to Peru in search of this Manuscript—did it really make sense? My intuition was dulled by the large breakfast, and I felt drowsy. I made some more coffee and meditated. Perhaps my soul was saying that it'd be wise to stay home and wait for 'The Three Tenors' to be shown on PBS a few *more* times if I wasn't sure about going to the jungle just yet. But the pull of the Manuscript was overwhelming. Soon I decided to start packing my bags and call my travel agent. He said he could get me on a plane to Peru if I could leave in three hours.

Three hours? I called another agent.

As I prepared to leave I kept saying to myself that this call from an old friend, this news about a manuscript in Peru, this dream, this big breakfast, was *not* just part of a mysterious coincidence—but was it? Little did I realize that I was about to enter a period of confusion about Insights that would last for a long, long time....

THE
LARGER
NOW

The stewardess awoke me to say that we'd be landing in Peru within 30 minutes. I was feeling a little queasy about having so quickly rearranged my life to pursue a bunch of Insights that might not even exist.

Lunch had already been served but I was starting to get hungry again, and started down the aisle toward the area where the food was prepared. I thought I could see if one of those apples was still uneaten—or just slightly eaten.

In the aisle I was astonished to pick up some fragments of a mumbled conversation between a heavyish passenger and a stewardess. It seemed as if every second word was 'Manuscript,' and every fourth word was 'Peru.' I couldn't make out the rest.

I returned to my seat to contemplate what I had heard, and decided to speak to the passenger just before we landed.

A few minutes later I approached him. "Pardon me, but I couldn't help overhearing you mention a Manuscript in Peru. Would this be *the* Manuscript?"

He seemed hesitant.

"Before I answer that," he responded, "could you tell me if you're *for* it or *against* it?"

"I've only heard about the First Insight," I responded, "and haven't even seen it yet, but I believe that I'm for it. I heard that it contains ancient wisdom about how to deal with extra weight on the physical body while also advancing the higher Self."

The gentleman seemed relieved.

"Yes, this sounds like the same Manuscript. I've come here to get as much information as I can. Would you like me to tell you about the Second Insight, or should I wait until you ask me about it?"

I was overwhelmed by my good fortune. "No—I mean yes—please tell me what you can."

"The Second Insight begins with looking at the entire history of our family lineage—photos would be best, but descriptions would do. When we get to see whether our ancestors were overweight it'll give us a larger perspective, or a perspective of who was large, in our genetic lineage.

"It also says that at the close of the second millenium—that's now—we will be able to see that entire history as a whole, and we will identify a particular *preoccupation* that developed during the latter half of this millenium, in what has been called the Modern Age. This preoccupation will finally reveal itself, and it will prove to be a preoccupation with the deposits that more and more routinely form in the back of the thighs and buttocks."

"Note that the Manuscript will—in the Third Insight— speak of *obsessiveness* as well as preoccupation. The preoccupation is with losing weight, but *the obsession is with the next meal.* Apparently we need to go back and forth over the past 1,000 years of history many times in order to resolve this.

"I remember one more thing about the Second Insight—and believe me, it'll be great when we all have copies of the Manuscript, because a lot can get lost by passing this on person-to-person, and if you've ever played 'telephone' you know what I mean—and that is that it says we sent some explorers out into history to bring back a complete report on what was really what. But they must have gotten lost, or maybe they stopped for a long bite—and they still haven't returned."

I was impressed by the gentleman's wisdom enough to arrange to follow along with him once we reached Peru.

Before landing I wondered about the past 1,000 years of humanity—and particularly, about my family's lineage. I visualized a large caveman meditating while munching on a primitive bowl of stone-ground chips or something. He was overweight, but he probably needed the extra padding to survive the winter. What was *my* excuse, I thought?

We landed, and, retrieving our baggage without any problem, left the airport quickly. The gentleman, who now introduced himself as Dobson, told me that a lot of people didn't want the Manuscript being made public, and we had to be very watchful to speak only to people who were *for* the Manuscript. I wished that everyone would just wear a button that said 'Yay' or 'Nay' so that we could have an easier time.

I hailed a taxi and headed toward Dobson's hotel. The next thing I knew, gunshots rang out and screams filled the air.

I jumped out of the cab yelling, "Don't shoot! I only know two Insights, and not very well!" and darted into an alleyway. A man whispered in my ear and scared the living daylights out of me.

"I'm Wil, and I know about the Manuscript. Let's drive to my friend's place."

My head was spinning with confusion, but I went with him. I finally centered out as we drove.

Wil glanced at me. "Do you have any questions?"

"I think I left my coffee maker on back in the States," I answered, still shaking with fright, "and I'm thinking of fast-forwarding my trip. Do you know a bunch of Insights that you can summarize for me?"

He responded in a low voice. "I can't address you by name—and nor can anyone else, for some reason—but I can say that the Insights need to be revealed and experienced one at a time. There are no short cuts. I've passed 'Go' eight times and am now searching for the Ninth Insight, and you're welcome to come with me on my search. I'm carrying about 20 extra pounds around the middle myself— so I'm motivated to find the last and, hopefully, most helpful Insight left behind by the Ancients. We'll share the driving and the preparation of snacks. What do you say?"

I hesitated, carefully considering all of my alternatives.

About three seconds later I said, "I'm in. Let's eat."

A
PLATTER
OF ENERGY

We rose at dawn and drove east all morning in virtual silence. Early on, Wil had mentioned that we would drive straight across the Andes and *probably* wouldn't get lost or run out of gas.

Apparently we were heading for a place called the Viciente Lodge, which his friend owned. It was a resort specializing in spiritual and culinary conferences, and they were preparing for an event this weekend entitled "Finding God in Godiva"— which, according to the brochure Wil had, featured "drumming, strumming, and empowering the higher taste buds." They also had research gardens, where one could experiment with new recipes.

When we arrived, Wil went to find his friend, and I walked around, admiring the expansive grounds. I heard a voice from behind me.

"Welcome to Shangri-La."

I turned to see an attractive woman. Her name was Sarah

and she could have been described as girlish except for her sheer size.

"Hi, Sarah," I said. "Is that a rolled-up Insight sticking out of your backpack?"

"Why, yes—it is. It's the Third."

"Can you tell me what it says?"

She hesitated.

"It describes a new understanding of the physical world. It says we humans will learn to perceive what was formerly an invisible type of energy—a new energy which forms the basis of all things, including ourselves. Human perception of this energy first begins with a heightened appreciation of—and becomes an obsession with—food, especially high-caloric food. This appreciation would enable humans to observe the energy fields around them. Once this occurred, it said, then our understanding of the physical universe would quickly transform. For instance, we would begin to eat more food of every kind, and we would become conscious that certain localities—for example, salad bars—radiate more energy than others, the highest energy coming from those that also have a dessert bar...."

She then revealed to me that the whole revolution in physics was inspired by two forces: quantum mechanics and Albert Einstein.

"Originally, we accepted Energy = MC^2 as a mysterious group of letters and numbers that only smart people could understand. But here at Viciente it was discovered in the kitchen that the real equation is Energy = Massive Calories, in square pans. Unfortunately, most scientists and priests don't take this seriously. Here, read it for yourself."

I started reading, but Sarah had more to say.

"The Manuscript says that beauty is also a powerful barometer of energy—and that if you develop your awareness you'll be able to *see* that beauty. I look at a gourmet dinner with all the trimmings and I see beauty. When I look at a five-decker sandwich that Dave Thomas conjured up with his customers the beauty is there, too, though it's often hidden under lots of pickles."

I promised that I would try to develop my awareness.

I sauntered further into the gardens in search of beauty when suddenly I saw the beautiful form of a woman who, though not exactly svelte, had a beautiful smile—in fact, I was taken by her immediately. We spoke long enough for me to discover that her name was Marjorie. Then she went to mingle with some friends. Sarah returned and asked me to follow her to an area where several people were staring at some *extremely* large stalks of corn.

"What are they doing?" I asked.

"They're giving their energy to the corn to help it grow. If you look at it from a certain angle, you can actually see it happening. It helps if you're a vegetarian."

It probably would help if I was from the Starship Enterprise too, I thought to myself, being careful to hide my disbelief from Sarah.

"Yes... well... I *think* I can almost see it."

Sarah introduced me to her friend Phil, and the three of us spent the afternoon looking between our fingers for beauty.

After agreeing to meet Sarah at 6 A.M. for breakfast, I went back to the lodge to see what was on tap for the evening. I discovered that traditional Peruvian entertainment was not offered at this unusual resort—but that, because it catered to spiritual seekers, a full complement of Angel workshops was available. Among them were "Discovering the Angel in You," "Finding Our Guardian Angels," and "Be an Angel and Help Me Finish These Leftovers—I Hate to Throw Them Out."

After my morning rendezvous with Sarah—during which I needed to get one more look at that corn—it was time to leave Viciente. As Wil and I drove away, I felt depressed. To my surprise, Wil laughed!

"It's a normal reaction," he said. "The food at Viciente is the best between here and the Seventh Insight. But don't be despondent. I put in a huge order to go."

I looked behind our jeep, and, sure enough, a U-Haul trailer was in tow. I suddenly felt a lot better.

As we drove through the Peruvian countryside Wil revealed a small coming attraction of the Fourth Insight. He said that sometimes humans unconsciously compete for this new form of energy—and may even compete for food itself, as this is the key that *unlocks* the energy—and that terrible conflict can result.

I held on tight to my burrito as I responded.

"Please tell me more."

THE
STRUGGLE
FOR PORTIONS

With all the talk about Insights, and so much bouncing in a jeep through rough terrain, I was fatigued.

All Wil could do was tell me again that the Manuscript is very enthusiastic about coincidences. I *had* to notice them... I *had* to notice them... I *had* to notice....

Just then we passed an overweight man on the side of the road who looked a *lot* like someone I knew. Wil had me so worked up over coincidences that for a moment early this morning—when I was getting dressed—I thought it was a coincidence that my driver's license had *my* picture on it and was in *my* wallet.

But, now, seeing a man who really reminded me of another man—well, this might be the real thing.

We turned around and drove back to meet the familiar-looking man. His name was Reneau, and we all liked each other so much that the three of us decided to share his campsite. We were to have dinner together and listen to Reneau obsess about conflict. He had read the Manuscript—that is, all but the rumored Ninth Insight—and so it seemed that he could help us get closer to our goal.

At about 7:00 P.M. we met and walked to the restaurant. The proprietors who ran the establishment—and their young daughter—seemed to be on edge.

We were told that the dinner would consist of several Peruvian classics—and all three of us were completely enthused. We seemed to be doing some significant male bonding.

Soon, the sweet young girl entered slowly with our Peruvian soup. The mother kept saying *"Slowly...slowly...it's* so hot!" The father, who was cooking in the kitchen, kept saying *"Quickly...quickly...it'll* get cold!"

In frustration, the young girl suddenly unloaded her tray upside down in my lap, shouted some obscene-sounding Spanish words at her parents, and then screamed something in my face that must have meant "Here's some energy on your lap, bub!"

Back at the campsite, we were relaxing. Wil said "It's been almost 10 minutes since anyone said anything about the Insights. I'll jump in."

"Let's focus on..." He paused, counting silently on his fingers. "...the *Fourth* Insight. Did you notice how energy is being pushed around like so much salami? For instance, the Peruvian family in the restaurant was giving us—and each other—bad vibrations from the moment we chose the inexpensive wine, and it didn't let up. Did you two see the way they dominated that poor girl?

"The Manuscript says that an energy field radiates from people, and, just as important, flows *between* people. It is the same with food. When one person dominates another, varying quantities of food may be sucked from the plate of the one who is being dominated. This may occur in a socially acceptable form, as in, 'Ooh, that looks good. May I have a taste?' or a more aggressive form, such as, 'You're not going to finish that, are you?' The result is always the same—a sense of power and fulfillment."

Wil then summarized the Insights. "In the First Insight, it spoke of an uneasiness caused by getting distended. In the Second Insight, it speaks of a preoccupation with dimples in the back of the thighs. In the Third Insight, the preoccupation is ignored, and it speaks of a new energy—an obsession with good food, remember? In the Fourth Insight, people might start throwing this food at each other, just like the young girl did in the restaurant—though the Manuscript says that usually a person knows another person pretty well before throwing this new form of energy at him. There's also a struggle for a decent-sized serving of anything, do you recall? In the Fifth Insight, we'll look at alternative sources of these foods, and previews of where to buy comfortable, looser, larger clothes.

"One other thing that the Manuscript speaks about is the importance of learning how to 'grasp,' such as in, 'do you grasp *this* Insight?' or 'do you grasp *that* Insight?' It says that it's much better to 'grasp it' than it is to 'get it' or 'understand it.'"

I felt dizzy from the overload of the new information, and wanted to go hide in my room and center myself. I wished that Marjorie was with me, and that if she *were* with me I wished that we could go out to a nice restaurant, and then perhaps talk about

'Bringers of the Dawn,' and then make passionate love to the strains of Enya, or even while 'The Three Tenors' was on—so at least I wouldn't have to *watch* it again, even if we did have to listen to it.

We awoke the next morning ready to go to Cula. We looked around the room to make sure that we hadn't left any energy behind and set out. Wil pointed out that "virgin forests converge in a 'v' at the vortex." It sounded to me like a New Age version of "the rain in Spain lies mainly on the plain." I didn't ask him for clarification because we were coming into Cula.

As soon as we drove into town I spotted Marjorie, and Wil and I invited her to join us for dinner. She agreed, and we found a small, out of the way place. I was surprised to see a small line of type on the menu under the name of the restaurant that read, "We Speak Manuscript."

Once seated, I tried to convince Marjorie to travel with us instead of with Jensen, an archaeologist whose camp she'd been staying in. I was concerned about his questionable reputation, so we visited him after we ate—I wanted to verify for myself just how ominous he was. He was *very* ominous: One of the ugly things he said was that he was prepared to trade his soul, and his mother's soul, for the movie and television rights to his planned epic 'The Nine Insights.' He offered us all bit parts as poor native Peruvians begging for spare energy fields.

THE
MESSAGE OF
THE BREADSTICKS

I arose early the next morning. Wil and I were ready to leave Cula, when he suggested that we look for Marjorie. Wil didn't trust Jensen—his men had guns, and he was on a power trip to keep all the Insights for himself.

I spotted Marjorie just as more shots rang out. We ran into the forest, but pretty soon we were separated, and Wil was in trouble, too.

I ran up into the mountains, worried about them, myself, and Peru's general reputation as a tourist spot. I ran and ran, and soon began to sweat profusely. I realized that if I could have the discipline to work out like this at home a couple of times a week at the gym, I wouldn't need the rest of the Insights.

Soon I ran to a dead end, and in one terrifying moment I knew that I was facing death. My whole life flashed before me. I thought of my early years, before I became interested in spiritual things. I was innocent and so caught up in the pleasures of the world—ego, worldly success, sexual conquests. These had been

17

my gods before I'd ever even *heard* expressions like 'inner child' or 'love-offering.'

I remember being introduced to the concepts of Eastern religion, and learning the importance of no-mindedness. I would meditate and listen to Ravi Shankar.

Then there had been my years in 'A Course in Miracles,' where I struggled with being a student *and* a teacher at the same time. Maybe if I would have taken some remedial classes for both I wouldn't be facing death so early.

Just as I had given up hope I realized that I had eluded the soldiers, and was safe for now! I started to feel a little light-headed, and then a little more so....

Then I felt a spinning sensation, and when I looked up into the sky, it almost seemed like it was wallpaper that I could cut and paste. It also seemed completely feasible that I could fly or merge with the sun—and that I was, after all, just pure light energy. I suddenly saw how the first four Insights tied into each other, how the entire history of evolution was all connected. The very cells of my body seemed somehow different—unreal—as if I were just a bunch of hydrogen and protons and....

I hadn't experienced anything like this since my trip to Jamaica, when I had smoked something herbal with a group of locals.

I sat down on some rocks to gather my atoms and neutrons. Suddenly I began to see the *evolution* of my body since childhood—it was like looking into prehistory, with bubbling lava and everything.

I saw myself as a young child at Sunday School, before I

had ever heard the word "overweight." I wore regular-sized clothes and won all the foot races in the church yard.

My mind raced backward and forward in time. Now I was a pre-teen, dressing up to go to the dance, starting to notice that Chubby Checker was built not entirely unlike myself. And my resemblance to my parents was becoming more pronounced.

The science of evolution had always bored me, but now my mind was racing around at full throttle. I saw myself as a full-grown adult, becoming interested in spiritual matters, but also becoming quite a bit wider in the hips. How did I get stuck with this inner program, and would it ever change?

Now evolution shot past the past, past the present, and into the future. I started to see my atoms working out on a Stairmaster at the gym, and my body slowly—over eons of evolutionary time/space matter—get just a little lighter, and lighter still. The eating of mass quantities had not changed, it seemed, but the effect on my waistline did. I saw that Charlene and Marjorie were also lighter, and so was Wil—he hardly looked at all like Dom DeLuise in 'Fatso' any more. Light was emanating from all of us....

I was suddenly awakened from my mind-altered experience by the sound of jeeps—with soldiers and guns. I froze, and I didn't dare move until a rather portly priest walked up to me and introduced himself as Father Sanchez.

This priest seemed like someone I could trust. He saw the "Looking for Insight Five" button on my lapel and didn't flinch. Instead he handed me a copy of the Insight, explaining that I could have it for a week, but would be charged a fee if I returned it with bullet holes in it.

I asked Father Sanchez to describe the Fifth Insight.

He obliged. "So long as we are deluded into thinking that the only way we can get more food is from others—others' refrigerators, others' pantries, even others' plates—we will continue to be constantly aggressing upon them. But as soon as we see that we can get food from a higher, bigger source—like Sam's Warehouse, if we can use the larger quantities—we will then be free of this conflict. With enough cash, or an approved bank card, or a local check with proper ID, we will have access to all the food we'll ever need.

"The Manuscript does state one warning relating to warehouse buying—it says that a 10 gallon jar of mayonnaise might not fit on the door of your refrigerator. Interpret this any way you'd like."

I admired Father Sanchez. He was able to rattle off the Insights in the right order at will, could wear loose clothes to work, and he regularly visited the power centers of Machu Picchu like it was nothing.

Soon Sanchez left, first saying to me that it was okay to hang out with the overweight priests, as they were *pro*-Manuscript. About noon, several of them began preparing a long table of food. I helped myself to a sumptuous plate. We sat in ecstatic silence, eating. Then a priest turned to me.

"Food is the first way of gaining energy."

"No kidding, Father," was my immediate response. I was happy that I finally had a way of relating to the 'energy' obsession so prevalent in these parts of Peru.

CLEANING
THE
PLATE

Sanchez was driving the jeep through the Andes mountains, and I was terrified of heights. When I saw that the narrow road we were traversing was higher than the clouds, I spoke with God in my prayers—I hadn't been so frightened since hearing a rumor that 'Yanni in Concert: Live at the Acropolis' might still have 16 more showings slotted this year. Sanchez had made a comment about 'control dramas' which had piqued my curiosity but I didn't dare suggest that he think about anything but safe driving principles right now.

We saw two pleasantly plump people ahead, and stopped. Sanchez pointed out the woman. "That's Julia. She was named for Julia Childs, a woman her mother emulated."

When we were safely away from the steep mountain drops, I asked Father Sanchez to tell me about the control dramas.

He was hesitant for a change.

"The Sixth Insight addresses what the Manuscript calls a clear awareness of your natural relationship to food. According to the Manuscript we all must spend as much time as necessary going through this process of "cleaning the plate"—that is, resolving our important issues. Most of us have a pattern we have to transcend, but once we do, we can proceed to eat what we want, and as much as we want of it.

"These patterns, or *control dramas*, as the Manuscript calls them, are subconscious ways in which we position ourselves in relation to all the food around us. There are four dramas— Intimidator, Interrogator, Aloof and Poor Me—which manifest as follows:

"The first is 'Intimidator,' which manifests itself whenever one individual threatens another, either verbally or physically, forcing them to hand over all or part of their dinner in order to gain their energy. Statements such as 'You're eating us out of house and home!' or 'I can't believe you *ordered* that!' or 'Give me that!' are signs that the Intimidator is present.

"The second is 'Interrogator.' People who use this means of gaining a meal set up a drama of asking questions and probing into another person's world with the specific purpose of finding something wrong. Once they do, they criticize this aspect of the other's life. 'Where did you learn to eat like that?' and 'You ordered *what*!?' are the utterings of the Interrogator.

"The third control drama is 'Aloof'—a more passive, defensive role. This drama comes to light whenever we are feeling put upon by others, and respond by withdrawing, looking mysterious and secretive. Confronted by the Intimidator or the Interrogator, the Aloof person will respond with retorts like 'I'm not sure if there *is* any turkey left to take home with you,' or 'Well...we *might* have a little more potatoes and gravy left.' The aim is to keep the aggressor off-balance and guessing. The Aloof person may choose not to answer at all, but just point to his or her closed mouth while chewing.

"The fourth drama is the 'Poor Me' drama—which unfolds when someone tells you all the horrible, fattening things they've eaten, implying that perhaps you are responsible. 'Why didn't you *stop* me?' is a common cry, then suggesting that if you refuse to help this overeating will continue. This type of person is seeking control at the most passive level.

"There were actually originally several more dramas: there was the 'Terminator', also known as the 'Poor You' type—who would out-and-out kill you and abscond with your dinner as you walked away from a take-out window; the 'Procrastinator'— who would invite you to dinner at his home and then take so long to prepare it that you'd leave before it was served and go to a restaurant, leaving twice the food for him; and the 'Fat You' type—who would buy you 5 pounds of chocolates for your birthday, hug you, and exclaim 'God, I can hardly get my arms around you anymore!' But these additional dramas eventually disappeared from the dynamics of human history as our whole world culture evolved to a higher level."

We were back on the road by now. Father Sanchez said that we'd be stopping off to see his friend Father Carl—who sounded like another ample man of the cloth. "He's an expert at seeing everyone's control dramas," Sanchez offered, "and, in fact, is obsessive. I remember him once talking to his goat, suggesting that the animal's father was a 'Poor Me' type. We're not always sure about Father Carl."

When I met him in person, Father Carl was true to his reputation. He suggested I get clear on my control drama by identifying those of my parents, and then integrate all the different dramas of East and West, up and down, and to and fro—and come up with a higher meaning for why my suit size was so large compared with my height in inches. He said that if we can discover the Ninth Insight we may solve the mystery of where all this global weight was heading, and how the Earth can live with it comfortably without annexing additional planets at this time.

Sanchez drove up suddenly. "We have to return to the mission. Sebastian's troops are looking for the Manuscript."

Sanchez then handed me a copy of the Sixth Insight.

"Read this, and then decide if you want to join us."

I read the entire text in less than thirty minutes, and finally understood that in order to take advantage of coincidences we had to wake up to who we really were underneath all these dramas and issues. I also realized that I couldn't remember what the Third Insight was for all the tea in China.

Father Sanchez and Father Carl returned and stared at me, trying to observe my energy fields. I suppressed my daydreams of an 'El Grande' burrito with everything on it, and tried to concentrate on love, beauty and coincidences.

ENLARGING
THE
CLOTHES

If someone would have told me six months ago—when I was trying to make my way through my aerobics class at the YMCA—that some day I'd be taking lessons in Peru in raising my energy by seeing beauty, breathing, and feeling love, I'd never have believed it.

But here I was with Father Sanchez and Father Carl doing just that.

"*See beauty*, two, three, four. *See beauty*, two, three, four. *Breathe*, two, three, four. *Breathe*, two, three, four. *Feel love*, two, three, four. *Feel love*, two, three, four...."

Father Sanchez explained that the Seventh Insight focused on how to raise energy, staying alert to inner guidance, consciously evolving, coincidences—of course—and how to clothe our bodily temples while all this development is going on.

Mention of this last element struck me as relevant—while I was doing the energy-raising exercises I received the inner guidance that I was going to have to go back to my tailor for more alterations if I expected to walk normally any more in these pants.

Father Sanchez tutored me in acquiring energy and consciously engaging evolution. He encouraged me to remember my basic life question—the one my parents gave me. I was confused, because my parents mostly wanted to know if I was acting like a 'nice young gentleman' and had good table manners. *Surely* my life must be about something more....

I decided to go forward, like most of the people driving jeeps here these days, and find the remaining Insights. I just had to get used to getting up in the morning and looking for beauty instead of a strong cup of coffee.

I proceeded in Father Carl's truck in search of my next alert awareness. It was already 10:30 A.M. and I'd had only one breakfast, so I pulled off the road in front of two modest Peruvian eating establishments. I now sat at a crossroads of sorts, unable to decide which one to go into. I thought about what the two Fathers said—but couldn't see a special glow coming from either direction. I tried to induce a love state surrounding either restaurant, but to no avail. Finally I opened the door and realized that all the good smells were coming from the one on the left, and went in without a further thought.

A little while later I saw that I was approaching a roadblock, and pulled into the bushes. I met a man whose substantial girth I recognized from Viciente—it was Phil! He told me that Viciente had been raided by the police. They confiscated all copies of the Manuscript and quarantined the high-energy corn.

Phil was telling me about the paper he was writing on Manuscript-Induced Insanity when, suddenly, the police were upon us. I was led down the hill and told to get into one of the military vehicles.

We rode until midnight, when we reached the minimum-security prison. To my surprise, I was treated kindly. At 11:00 P.M. I closed the door to my cell myself and drifted off to sleep.

My dream was vivid. In it, I was lost in a torrential rainstorm deep in the forest. I was washed into the river, but grabbed on to a rubber life raft. I saw Marjorie float by and pulled her into the raft. Then we saw Oprah Winfrey and pulled her in, too. The three of us wept with happiness that we were saved. Then we saw Richard Simmons. We pulled him in, and told him how thin he looked. Moments later, we sank to the bottom of the river.

I woke up startled. Pablo, a young round-shaped Indian guard, assured me that I was having a bad dream, but that that was good. He explained that he had gotten a job teaching the Seventh Insight, and that I might consider signing up for the 4-week course. I said that this was impossible, so he told me that the Insight talked about dreams of food and how they come to tell us something important.

His words rang in my ears. He hadn't said much, but since it was free, it was okay for now. I went to lunch.

In the lunchroom I saw Marjorie, and went straight to her table. Peruvian prisons are extremely humane, I thought; I didn't expect to see chips and salsa served while we were waiting to give our order.

After lunch a heavyish man named Father Costous interrogated me, suggesting that the Church was still the final authority on everything. He flew into a rage several times.

When I returned to my cell I asked Pablo what else the Seventh Insight said about dreams.

"The Manuscript says that dreams and daydreams about food are common, especially for a 'full-figured,' 'goddess-sized,' 'queen-sized,' or 'Queen Mary-sized' spiritual person," he said. "They guide us, usually to our next meal. It also says that these thoughts come to us very quickly, and we must take an observer position for a while or we'll blow up like a blimp."

"But what about dreams of outrageously fattening desserts?" I interjected. "Didn't you say that something bad can be good?"

"That's covered too," Pablo said. "The Seventh Insight says fattening food images must be halted as soon as they come, or you'll have to dream up a shirt with a bigger collar to wear to work next week."

Pablo also implied that everybody's got some kind of message for everybody else. He wanted to know what message I had for him, what message Father Costous had for me, and what message Wil had for Marjorie's Aunt Martha in Dubuque, Iowa. I didn't know the answers to any of his questions—and was actually relieved when the guard came and led me away.

THE
INTERPERSONAL
ADS

I followed the soldier up the steps and into the bright sunshine, with confusion in my head. What did Pablo mean when he said beware of *additions* as it related to relationships?

Then, as we walked toward the parking lot, to my great surprise and excitement I saw Marjorie sitting in the back of one of the military vehicles. Suddenly I recalled how my social life back in the States had been such a challenge. I had placed a few ads, but to no avail—being spiritual, I couldn't lie and say that I was weight/height proportional. Now I was aware of how much I appreciated Marjorie. Just then a soldier grabbed my arm and shoved me into the seat next to her. I was pleased at this serendipity. It could also have been seen as a coincidence, but I was going to need six lifetimes as it was to explore the meaning of the coincidences I had encountered since arriving in Peru, so I thought I'd treat this as something else.

I hugged Marjorie, and suddenly wished that I was eating fruit and whipped cream from her body, like in *9-1/2 Weeks*. My fantasy was interrupted by a sudden explosion that sent us flying out of the jeep. In an instant, my life flashed before me, and I tried to recollect which Insight had predicted this kind of thing, and if this was yet another coincidence—and then I thought, what's the difference, dammit, just run! I realized that the escape would have much more meaning if Marjorie came with me, so I grabbed her hand and ran down the Peruvian alleyway looking for a place to hide.

We darted into a doorway, and then into a hallway from which we could see a big Peruvian living room where a heavy-set dark-haired woman and her diapered baby seemed almost to be awaiting our arrival. She beckoned us to come in. I said to myself that there's no way that this woman will know anything about the Manuscript or the Insights.

"You two must hide!" she commanded. And she whispered to her infant, who immediately came crawling in our direction and motioned to us—with spit drooling down her face—to follow her.

When we laughed at this, the dark-haired woman turned to us angrily.

"If you're looking for the Manuscript, I suggest you read the Eighth Insight as soon as you find it. It speaks about how to relate to children."

"What exactly does the Manuscript say?" I said, for the umpteenth time this week.

"The Eighth Insight talks about many things. It talks about people relating to people, people relating to children, people relating to big dogs without collars and name tags, and of many other things—such as how to project your voice in a noisy restaurant, and how to avoid additions."

I was confused. "Additions?"

She continued. "Reneau taught me this. He said that the idea of additions, as used in the Manuscript, explains why power struggles arise in romantic relationships. We've always wondered what causes the bliss and euphoria of love to end, to suddenly turn into conflict, and now we know."

Before she could finish, the woman—who said her name was Karla—went to check the oven. I seized my opportunity and kissed Marjorie passionately. It was wonderful! Then Karla returned and continued speaking.

"When two individuals marry, they're usually attracted physically, as well as emotionally, intellectually, and, hopefully, spiritually. In the areas of the emotion, the intellect, and the spirit, additions *work*—that is, more and more is successfully *added* to each of these centers. The intellectual body may add an interest in politics, sports, or music where none existed before. Likewise, the emotional aspect of an individual may add facets of deeper love or compassion to feelings which can be shared with the beloved partner. The spiritual body may add faith or 'inner knowing' to its lineup.

"But the Manuscript says that it's in the area of the physical body that there must be, generally speaking, as much *subtraction* as there is *addition,* or eventually a surplus, or overage, will result. If the beloved *adds* five pounds, he or she is going to want to *subtract* five pounds. If the beloved adds five pounds, but subtracts only four pounds, that'll be okay for a while. It depends on the intensity and magnitude of each addition, and the hoped-for subtraction of equal magnitude. One way to avoid additions is to always say 'no' to a waiter when he asks if you'll be wanting to add an appetizer or special garlic bread to your order. Pray to Mother Mary that the meal doesn't automatically come with all the additions.

"One final thing which the Eighth Insight covers is *integration.* It's pretty complex, but basically, it means that we should integrate our male and female aspects, and, at the same time, integrate the aspects of the same-sexed parent and the opposite-sexed parent to the new integrated inner you. It can get pretty crowded in there, I assure you. I had seven sisters and fourteen brothers, and made the mistake of reading the Eighth Insight just at a time in my life when I was getting pretty spiritually clear. I had to integrate these twenty-one siblings—the male *and* female aspect of each—with my integration of both inner sexes of both parents, and then integrate all that with my previously integrated inner male and female Selves which had become a single Self.

"I never fully recovered from this mega-integration, and I've been in counseling ever since; my therapist uses a modality which un-integrates for the first 6 months, and then re-integrates, but this time using a sort of 'Teflon for the mind' technique which prevents sticking if there are too many energies involved."

I looked at Marjorie, who hadn't yet gotten past the Third Insight—and felt compassion for her as she was still trying to understand what Karla's baby was saying.

The next morning, I suspected that I may have received some of the Eighth Insight out of sequence, and wasn't sure how to resolve that. Then Julia offered to take me to Iquitos to look for

Wil, who was looking for the Ninth Insight. Marjorie told me that she was going back to Kansas to be with normal-sized corn, and was upset when I told her that I couldn't go with her. I knew I had to go onward, and we said goodbye for now.

I told Julia I would join her if she promised not to ask me for the details of *every single* daydream—especially the ones I had late at night. I also cited the Human Rights Act, demanding that she limit her suggestions about sending or receiving energy to a maximum of 10 per hour.

We set out for Iquitos immediately, with Julia discussing control dramas and important messages at every mile marker. I recalled that Pablo, too, was obsessed with important messages. I wished I could put Julia together with Pablo and let them go off into 'important message' heaven.

To our great and happy surprise, after driving for a long time, we found Father Sanchez, and had a wonderful reunion. Sanchez indicated that he—and I, if I decided to go with him—would actually go right into Cardinal Sebastian's mission to try to convince him to release the Manuscript. He also hoped we could find the fabled Ninth Insight.

Sanchez gave me one final warning about the group dynamics that awaited us. "Speak only when it's your turn."

"And don't eat everything that's offered to you," added Julia. "Some people get inflated in a group. They feel the burst of energy that comes from the treats, and keep on eating long after they should have passed the tray to the next person."

With that warning we headed north into the jungle.

THE
EMERGING
BEST SELLER

Sanchez and I drove through the jungle toward Sebastian's mission. We wanted to talk about the Ninth Insight, but hadn't discovered it yet, so we reminisced about earlier ones. He was really hung up on energy, though.

"Uh, oh... there's another fork in the road," Sanchez pointed out.

Fortunately Phil was standing in the road to tell us that the soldiers were to the left, so we didn't have to look for love or energy glows to point the way. To our surprise, we came upon Dobson and realized that we had a foursome if we wanted to go play some golf at 'Vizcaya Iquitos,' a golf community just down the road. But we were much more interested to hear the big news that Phil had actually seen some of the Ninth Insight.

"Phil, what did it say?" we asked in unison.

Phil was animated. "I've only seen part of it, but according to the Manuscript, the population of 500-year-old trees will surpass the human population in the next millenium. There'll be a great shift, and we'll be guided by our intuitions in all we do. We'll be paid by others for telling them the truth, and as our vibrations get higher and higher, we'll transform into our *light bodies* and soon find—get this—that we can eat all we want and the calories won't stick."

Calories won't stick! We were thrilled to hear this part of the final prophecy. Father Sanchez and I soon left in a state of exhilaration, and drove toward our date with destiny.

As he drove, I asked Sanchez what he was thinking about.

He paused. "I was thinking about Sebastian."

At that moment, I began having another one of those prophetic daydreams. In it, I came to confession, only to find that Cardinal Sebastian and three tough-looking men with machine guns were all behind the screen. I was reluctant to say "Father, I have sinned" under these conditions, so I just said, "Father, I need advice."

"Yes, what is it, my son?"

"I may have read the Manuscript."

"What!? Which Insights?"

"Possibly One through the first part of Nine."

"My son, are you for or against it?"

At that point, I nervously changed the subject. "Father, are we having those divine fried corn-things again at lunch today?"

I woke up from my daydream in a sweat.

Father Sanchez saw my discomfort, and intuitively said, "Don't worry. Your daydreams aren't *always* prophetic. This may not even be revealed until the next book, but the Manuscript will say that—like on network TV in America—you can yank a pilot if it doesn't seem right, and rewrite the script, so to speak."

I was relieved.

"Thanks, Father Sanchez. I'll try again."

But before I could, Sanchez told me that we were arriving at Cardinal Sebastian's mission.

We walked into the lavish building and were escorted to Sebastian's study. I realized that it was here that the Manuscript's fate would be decided. Sebastian was standing near the window as he addressed Sanchez.

"My son," Sebastian said, "What you say to me, and how you say it, will influence the entire resolution of this long and arduous journey of mankind since amoebic times.

"You have a choice of either answering to a long list of serious allegations—or you can focus on a single essay question entitled "Why Cardinal Sebastian Should Not Be Afraid to Let the People of the World Read the Manuscript."

He threw us off guard with these words.

Sanchez motioned to me that he wasn't too good at true-false questions, and would go for the essay question.

"Cardinal Sebastian, I'll bare my soul—though if I'd bare my stomach, I'd probably get my point across better. You, I, Father Carl, Marjorie, and most of the spiritually oriented people on the planet at this time are chronically overweight, and we're feeling conflicted about it. The ancient Manuscript which we've been running up and down the hills of Peru looking for promises to resolve this dilemma—and show us the way to a *lighter future.* If you can remember back to when you were captain of the St. Brendan's of Peru high school track team, you'll remember the joy of lightness and agility. If you'll allow the Manuscript to be made public, we'll *all* be able to reclaim this original state."

As Sanchez finished, I saw tears in Sebastian's eyes.

"I'll always be a fatty," he exclaimed, blowing his nose, "and so will both of you. No Manuscript! Now go on, get outta here before I outlaw Spandex in Peru!"

Sanchez and I ran out of the mission and into the woods to find Wil and Julia, who—I would soon find out—had found the rest of the Ninth Insight. They were nowhere to be found.

"Over here!" a voice exclaimed, but we didn't see anyone.

"I'm invisible!" the voice continued. As we moved toward the sound I bumped into a large invisible stomach. It was Wil!

Then I noticed Julia, who was completely glowing, and whose head was looking a lot like a GE 600-watt bulb. She addressed us happily.

"The rest of the Ninth Insight says that all of us, overweight or not, are evolving into our light bodies as our cumulative vibration reaches a high note. No matter what our size or shape, we'll all *weigh nothing*—we'll stop worrying about our clothes, and throw them away! Don't you see? We can't all do it yet, but the role of the Ninth Insight is to create that confidence."

Without warning, machine gun fire was all around us. We were all captured except Wil, who couldn't be seen, and who indicated to us that he was heading into town for his first worry-free meal—and would report back to us on his findings.

My energy levels went haywire in the weeks that followed my capture. I met up with Father Carl, who was still helping the guards sort out their control dramas.

"What a coincidence this is!" he exclaimed when he saw me. He continued intently. "I've got good news and bad news. Which would you like first?"

"Well... let's start with the bad news," I answered.

"The bad news is that the Manuscript is *kaput*, gone. Nada left. The good news is that we've memorized it by now, right? We *have* to get this message out to everyone—even if we become invisible like Wil—and it may not be easy, because most people don't trust voices without bodies."

Father Carl also made a vague mention about a possible Tenth Insight. I thought about Charlene for some reason, and made a mental note *not* to meet her for any more reunions.

The officials finally decided that it was okay for me to leave the country, and took me to the airport. I was exhilarated by the wisdom that the Ninth Insight had revealed; I couldn't wait to get home and start passing the message to *everyone* who was ready for it—even though I'd probably have to quit my job to have enough time.

I decided to fly first class on Peruvian World Airlines— their ads promised a seven-course gourmet dinner. I leaned back and loosened my belt past the third new notch—and knew it would never, never return.

Appendix

Ideal Weights in Light Bodies - Women

height	small frame	medium frame	large frame
4'11" *	0 lbs.	0 lbs.	0 lbs.
5'	0 lbs.	0 lbs.	0 lbs.
5'1"	0 lbs.	0 lbs.	0 lbs.
5'2"	0 lbs.	0 lbs.	0 lbs.
5'3"	0 lbs.	0 lbs.	0 lbs.
5'4"	0 lbs.	0 lbs.	0 lbs.
5'5"	0 lbs.	0 lbs.	0 lbs.
5'6"	0 lbs.	0 lbs.	0 lbs.
5'7"	0 lbs.	0 lbs.	0 lbs.
5'8"	0 lbs.	0 lbs.	0 lbs.
5'9"	0 lbs.	0 lbs.	0 lbs.
5'10"	0 lbs.	0 lbs.	0 lbs.
5'11" *	0 lbs.	0 lbs.	0 lbs.

* for heights under 4'11" or over 5'11", write to the publisher.

Ideal Weights in Light Bodies - Men

height	small frame	medium frame	large frame
5'4" *	0 lbs.	0 lbs.	0 lbs.
5'5"	0 lbs.	0 lbs.	0 lbs.
5'6"	0 lbs.	0 lbs.	0 lbs.
5'7"	0 lbs.	0 lbs.	0 lbs.
5'8"	0 lbs.	0 lbs.	0 lbs.
5'9"	0 lbs.	0 lbs.	0 lbs.
5'10"	0 lbs.	0 lbs.	0 lbs.
5'11"	0 lbs.	0 lbs.	0 lbs.
6'0"	0 lbs.	0 lbs.	0 lbs.
6'1"	0 lbs.	0 lbs.	0 lbs.
6'2"	0 lbs.	0 lbs.	0 lbs.
6'3"	0 lbs.	0 lbs.	0 lbs.
6'4" *	0 lbs.	0 lbs.	0 lbs.

* for heights under 5'4" or over 6'4", write to the publisher.

'Author Unknown'
may be reached
by writing or calling:

light-hearted books
Lumina Publishing
P.O. Box 7324
Daytona Beach Shores, FL 32116

(904) 258-5300